COUNTDOWN TO SPACE

THE MOON—
EARTH'S COMPANION IN SPACE

Michael D. Cole

Series Advisors:
Marianne J. Dyson
Former NASA Flight Controller
and
Gregory L. Vogt, Ed. D.
NASA Aerospace Educational Specialist

Enslow Publishers, Inc.

40 Industrial Road   PO Box 38
Box 398   Aldershot
Berkeley Heights, NJ 07922 Hants GU12 6BP
USA   UK

http://www.enslow.com

Library of Congress Cataloging-in-Publication Data

Cole, Michael D.
    The Moon : earth's companion in space / Michael D. Cole.
        p. cm. — (Countdown to space)
    Includes bibliographical references (p.   ) and index.
    ISBN 0-7660-1510-6
    1. Moon—Juvenile literature. [1. Moon.] I. Title. II. Series.
QB582.C47 2001
523.3—dc21   00-010021

Printed in the United States of America

10 9 8 7 6 5 4 3 2 1

To Our Readers: All Internet Addresses in this book were active and appropriate
when we went to press. Any comments or suggestions can be sent by e-mail to
Comments@enslow.com or to the address on the back cover.

Illustration Credits: Courtesy Calvin J. Hamilton, p. 9; © Corel
Corporation, p. 19; Enslow Publishers, Inc., p. 21; National Aeronautics
and Space Administration (NASA), pp. 4, 8, 11, 13, 14, 16–17, 23, 24, 27,
28, 29, 30, 32, 37, 39, 41.

Cover Illustration: NASA (foreground); Raghvendra Sahai and John
Trauger (JPL), the WFPC2 science team, NASA, and AURA/STScI
(background).

CONTENTS

Apollo 11 *explodes off the launchpad as it begins its journey to the Moon. In the capsule atop the rocket, Neil Armstrong, Edwin Aldrin, and Michael Collins were about to make history.*

1

One Small Step

It was July 20, 1969. Astronauts Neil Armstrong and Edwin Aldrin had guided the lunar module *Eagle* to a safe landing on the surface of the Moon. In his white spacesuit and helmet, Armstrong carefully made his way out of the spacecraft and down the lunar module's ladder. People all over the world watched as he paused at the base of the ladder, then took his first step onto the surface of the Moon.

"That's one small step for a man," Armstrong said, "one giant leap for mankind."[1]

Armstrong's "giant leap" was humanity's historic first step on a world other than Earth. Five more Apollo missions landed on the lunar surface. Each made further explorations of the Moon and conducted many experiments. Yet many important questions about the Moon remained unanswered. After six Apollo landings and many years of studying the Moon rocks brought back by the astronauts, scientists were still uncertain of many things.

Where did the Moon come from?

How was it formed?

How old is it?

Was the Moon once part of Earth?

Has the Moon always been in orbit around Earth?

Was the Moon originally an asteroid, captured long ago by Earth's gravity?

Despite the success of the Moon landings, the Apollo missions did not answer these questions fully.

In the 1990s and 2000s, robotic spacecraft were visiting the Moon again. The spacecraft carried new instruments that might give scientists further clues about how the Moon formed. Discovering the origin of the Moon could also reveal more of what the early solar system was like.

These explorations are only the latest in humanity's quest to learn about the Moon. Our ancestors began that search long ago, when they first looked up into the sky and wondered about our nearest neighbor in space.

2

Earth's Companion

The Moon is the only known natural body in space that travels along with Earth in its orbit around the Sun. The force of Earth's gravity and the Moon's own gravity hold the Moon in an orbit around our planet.

The Moon is closer to Earth than any other known natural object in space. It orbits Earth at an average distance of about 240,000 miles (385,000 kilometers). The next nearest planet, Venus, never gets closer than 26 million miles (42 million kilometers) from Earth.

The light we see from the Moon at night is light that the Moon reflects from the Sun. The closeness of the Moon, and the amount of sunlight it reflects to Earth, makes the Moon the largest and brightest object in the night sky. The Moon is often bright enough to be visible through part of the day as well. It was only natural that early civilizations would be fascinated by the Moon, and curious about its regular journeys through the sky.

Many ancient cultures regarded the Moon as a god or the home of a god. Khons, an Egyptian Moon-god, could chase away sickness and evil spirits. The ancient Greeks worshipped the Moon-goddess Selene. The Romans renamed the Moon-goddess Luna. The name Luna is the origin of the descriptive word *lunar*, which means

The light seen coming from the Moon is reflected sunlight.

"related to the Moon." For example, the spacecraft that landed people on the Moon was called the lunar module.[1]

The Babylonians and other early civilizations began using the Moon's journeys through the sky to measure time and keep track of the seasons. Knowledge about the length and change of seasons was important to these civilizations because it told them the best times at which to plant and gather their crops.[2]

The Moon is a giant ball of rock. It is 2,160 miles (3,476 kilometers) in diameter, making it about one-fourth the size of Earth. But it has only 1.25 percent of Earth's mass, which means it is only 1.25 percent as heavy as Earth.

The Moon's structure consists of a crust layer, a mantle, and probably a small iron core. The crust is as little as twenty miles thick in some places, and as much as sixty miles thick in others. It is made up mostly of volcanic rock called basalt. Below the crust is the mantle. The mantle makes up 90

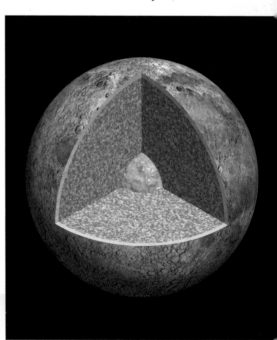

This image shows the Moon's crust, mantle, and core.

percent of the Moon's volume, and is about 800 miles (1,287 kilometers) thick.

Scientists are uncertain about the size of the Moon's core, or if it has a core at all. The latest evidence, however, suggests that the Moon probably has an iron core that is about 200 miles (322 kilometers) in radius.[3]

Terrae, Maria, and Craters

The three major features on the surface of the Moon are highlands (called terrae), the plains (called maria), and the many craters. The maria are the dark splotches that can be seen on the Moon from Earth. *Maria* is the Latin word for seas. Galileo, the first astronomer to look at the Moon with a telescope, mistakenly thought the dark areas were seas full of water. However, the maria were caused long ago by the impacts of large asteroids or comets, which caused the impact basins to be flooded with lava from the Moon's interior. These areas are smoother and have fewer craters because the impact and lava wiped all the old craters away.

The same side of the Moon always faces Earth. The far side of the Moon (the side we never see) has almost no areas of maria. The crust on the Moon's far side is generally thicker than on the near side. Scientists believe the thicker crust may have made it more difficult for asteroids or comets to punch through the crust and bring lava from the interior onto the surface to create areas of maria. The reason for the crust's difference in thickness has remained a mystery to scientists.[4]

The terrae are another major surface feature on the Moon. They are mountains, many of which have been pushed up along the rims of large impact craters. Because the terrae regions are high and have not been resurfaced,

The dark areas on this image of the Moon are impact basins, which were flooded long ago with lava. The image was taken in 1992 by the Galileo spacecraft on its way to Jupiter.

they show many more craters. The mountainous terrae regions include the uplifted rims and rifts of large craters, some rising more than 15,000 feet (4,500 meters) high.[5]

Craters are the most obvious features of the Moon. Photographs taken by telescopes and orbiting spacecraft show thousands of craters. But there are millions of smaller craters covering the surface of the Moon. These were first seen when spacecraft and astronauts flew close enough to the Moon's surface to make landings.

The major craters on the Moon measure from less than a mile wide to more than 700 miles (1,100 kilometers) wide. They were created throughout the Moon's history by the many impacts of meteorites, asteroids, and comets. Larger objects created larger craters. But not all craters on the Moon are alike. Craters have different structures depending on their size.

Simple craters less than twelve miles wide are shaped like a bowl and surrounded by a raised ring of ejected debris. Through a telescope, these craters look like they are deep hollows. This is an illusion created by the effect of shadows falling across the craters' raised walls. The floors of these craters are actually not very far below the surface of the surrounding lunar landscape.

Craters 12 to 120 miles wide are called complex craters. They have a flat floor with a surrounding ring of debris that slumps inward. At the center of these complex craters is a raised peak. The central peak is created many years after the initial impact, when the

Two complex craters on the Moon: Aristarchus (left) and Herodotus (right).

floor of the crater slowly rebounds from the impact's compression shock. Gravity causes the rim of the crater to slump inward, filling the crater with debris. This action makes the crater wider and more shallow.[6]

Craters larger than 120 miles are known as basins. They are similar in structure to complex craters. But instead of a raised peak at the center, basins have a smaller raised ring. The Moon's two largest basins have multiple rings around the center. The Mare Orientale, a crater more than 600 miles wide, has four ring structures within the main outer ring wall.[7]

Surface Dust

All of the Moon's surface is covered by a fine, gray dust called regolith. It was made by lunar rocks being bombarded for millions of years by small micrometeorites. The constant bombardment gradually reduced the lunar rocks to a dust. The regolith is so fine that the Apollo astronauts found it impossible to clean it off their spacesuits after their Moonwalks.

Astronaut John Young used a rake on the dusty surface of the Moon to collect samples of the Moon. Notice how the gray dust from the Moon discolored Young's spacesuit.

"It's so fine," explained *Apollo 16*'s John Young, "it's not like beach sand. It's not rounded particles. It's all impact particles, and they all have sharp corners, and if you put something on it, it never leaves."

"When people talk about long-duration operations on the Moon," he added, "the thing they better worry about is the dust."[8]

Unlike many mountains on Earth, the mountains on the Moon have no sharp or jagged peaks because of the bombardment of micrometeorites. Any cliffs that were once steep or ledges that were once sharp have become rounded over millions of years by micrometeorites pounding them into regolith.

Much of the information about the Moon's structure and surface was gained only after spacecraft and astronauts went there to explore. Many of the Moon's other features, however, can be observed from Earth. The nature of the Moon's orbit, for example, and the appearance of the Moon's various phases, can be observed by anyone. Chapter 3 explains how you can watch the Moon's path through space.

THE MOON

Diameter
2,160 miles (3,476 kilometers)

Mass
1 percent of Earth's mass

Gravity on surface
1/6 of Earth's gravity

Average speed of orbit around Earth
2,288 miles per hour
(3,681 kilometers per hour)

Average distance from Earth
240,000 miles (384,401 kilometers)

Temperature on dark side
-275° F to -300° F (-170° C to -185° C)

Temperature on sunlit side
266° F (130° C)

Estimated age
4.6 billion years

Time required to complete one orbit of Earth
27 days 8 hours

Time required to complete cycle of phases
29 days 13 hours

**Time it took Apollo astronauts
to reach the Moon**
about 2 1/2 days

**Number of astronauts who
have walked on the surface**
12

**Total amount of lunar rocks
brought back by Apollo astronauts**
842 pounds (383 kilograms)

Area of lunar surface covered by maria
17 percent

Area of lunar highlands
83 percent

Largest mare formation
Oceanus Procellarum (large lunar mare
covering 63,000 square miles)

3

Tides, Orbit, and Phases of the Moon

People who live near Earth's ocean shores need not see the Moon in the sky to know that it is there. Every day, they witness how the Moon and its orbit affect Earth's oceans.

The Moon is large enough and close enough to Earth to have its own gravitational effects on our planet. The Moon's gravity causes the oceans to bulge on two sides of Earth: one nearest to the Moon, and one on the opposite side. This effect creates the ocean tides. The Moon's gravity and Earth's daily rotation on its axis cause the tides to rise and fall. While two parts of Earth are experiencing high tide along its ocean shores, other parts of Earth are experiencing low tide. It is all because of the Moon's gravity.[1]

The Moon's Orbit

The Moon's orbit around Earth is not a circle. It is elliptical, or oval. During this orbit, the Moon comes as close as 221,000 miles (356,000 kilometers), and can be as far away as 253,000 miles (407,000 kilometers) from Earth. Although the Moon's distance changes by 32,000 miles (51,000 kilometers), the size of the Moon in the sky is always roughly the same to our eyes, no matter how close or far away it is from Earth.

Sometimes, however, our eyes are fooled about the size of the Moon. When we observe the Moon close to objects on a distant horizon, the Moon seems bigger. But it really is not. This is an optical illusion. When a tree

The Moon's gravity creates the daily tides on Earth.

on the distant horizon appears very small in front of the Moon, the effect makes the Moon by comparison appear much larger. But as the Moon rises farther above the horizon, the effect is lost. Without small, distant objects for our eyes to compare with the Moon's size, it no longer appears as big.[2]

The Phases of the Moon

Although the actual size of the Moon changes little in our eyes, its shape is a different story. Sometimes the Moon looks like a crescent. At other times it looks like a half-circle. There are also times when it appears perfectly round. These are the Moon's phases.

We see the Moon in phases because it is orbiting Earth. As we watch the Moon from Earth, the Moon's motion in the sky appears to be from east to west. But this motion is the result of Earth's rotation on its axis, which makes all objects in space, including the Sun, appear to move across the sky in that direction. The Moon actually orbits Earth from west to east. You can observe this motion easily by noting the Moon's position in relation to the pattern of stars behind it. If you observe the Moon one night, and again on the following night, you will notice that the Moon's orbit has carried it well to the east of the pattern of stars that surrounded it on the previous night. As the Moon's orbit continues in this direction, the Sun lights up different parts of the Moon you are looking at, creating phases.

When the Moon is at a position between the Sun and the Earth, the Moon is not visible to us. The reason is that the side of the Moon facing Earth is completely unlit by the Sun. This is called the New Moon.

Following the New Moon, the Moon's orbit carries it further east through our sky, and more and more of the Moon becomes lit by the Sun as seen from Earth. As more of the Moon becomes visible each night, it is said to be waxing. In the first seven nights, the Moon's shape progresses from a crescent to a half-circle, in which the

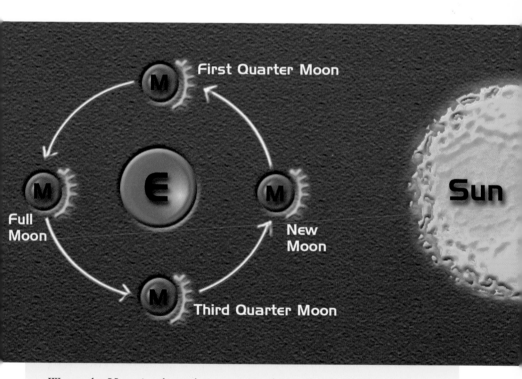

We see the Moon in phases because it is orbiting Earth. The Sun lights up different parts of the Moon as we are looking at it.

right half of the Moon is lit. The half-circle Moon is called the First Quarter Moon.

After First Quarter, the Moon's face continues to appear more circular each night. This is the gibbous phase. Because the lighted face of the Moon is growing larger, it is called a waxing gibbous Moon.

On about the fifteenth night after New Moon, the Moon reaches a position on the other side of Earth from the Sun. At that point, the face of the Moon is completely lit by the Sun. This is the Full Moon. In the fourteen nights that follow the Full Moon, we see less and less of the Moon's face lit by the Sun. This is the Moon's waning phase, which includes the waning gibbous Moon and the Third Quarter Moon.

The Moon's orbit eventually carries it back to a position between the Sun and Earth. It is again a New Moon, its lighted side facing away from Earth.[3]

The Moon completes one orbit in 27 days and 8 hours. But it takes two more days to complete its cycle of phases. Because the Earth has continued in its orbit around the Sun, the Sun is in a slightly different position in the sky than it was at the last New Moon. The change in the Sun's position means that the Moon must travel in its orbit this added distance before it can return to the New Moon phase. The 27-day-and-8-hour period in which the Moon completes one orbit is called a sidereal month. The 29-and-a-half-day period required to complete the cycle from New Moon to the next New

This image shows a crescent Moon, just before First Quarter Moon.

Moon is known as the synodic month.

The synodic month is about equal to a calendar month. The word *month* comes from the word *moon*. Our modern twelve-month calendar is based on the twelve trips the Moon takes around Earth in approximately one year.

While the phases cause our view of the Moon to change, we always see the same side of the Moon. Like Earth, the Moon rotates on its axis, like a basketball spinning on a fingertip. Earth rotates once on its axis every twenty-four hours, giving us our cycle of night and day. The Moon's rotation, however, is exactly as long as its orbit around Earth. This exact relation means that the same side of the Moon always faces Earth. We never see the other side, commonly called the far side.

It has been nearly four centuries since scientists first looked at the Moon with their telescopes. As telescopes improved, astronomers added to their knowledge of the Moon's many features. But because the Moon's rotation was in exact relation with its orbit, scientists and astronomers could not study the Moon's far side with telescopes. And without a closer study of the rock and other material on the Moon, scientists could only wonder where the Moon came from and how it was formed. By the 1960s, it was clear that these questions about the Moon could be answered only by going there.

Astronauts aboard Apollo 11 *photographed the far side of the Moon. This far side cannot be seen from Earth.*

4

Journeys to the Moon

The space age began in 1957 when scientists in the Soviet Union sent the first artificial satellite, *Sputnik,* into orbit around Earth. Beyond Earth-orbit, the next destination for spacecraft was the Moon.

The Soviet space program's *Luna 2* was the first man-made object to reach the Moon. *Luna 2* crashed, as planned, on the lunar surface in September 1959, proving that the Moon could be reached by spacecraft. One month later, *Luna 3* took the first pictures of the Moon's far side. The pictures surprised scientists, who had not expected the far side of the Moon to look so different from the side facing Earth. *Luna 3*'s images were the first to show the more highly cratered surface and lack of maria on the Moon's far side—evidence of the far side's thicker crust.[1]

In 1964 and 1965, the American spacecraft *Ranger 7*, *Ranger 8*, and *Ranger 9* all sent back pictures superior to those from *Luna 3*, before they too crashed onto the Moon. In 1966, the Soviet spacecraft *Luna 9* made the first soft landing, and sent back pictures directly from the surface of the Moon.

By 1966, five Lunar Orbiter spacecraft from the United States had completed a detailed mapping of nearly all of the lunar surface. The Lunar Orbiters were followed by five Surveyor spacecraft, the first American spacecraft to make soft landings on the Moon. While astronauts trained and prepared for the Apollo program to send humans to the Moon, scientists studied the Lunar Orbiter and Surveyor maps, looking for areas where the first astronauts could land.

Manned Missions to the Moon

Apollo 8 was the first manned flight to orbit the Moon. The astronauts did not land but flew their command module to the Moon and back, proving astronauts could get to the Moon and safely return. *Apollo 9* and *Apollo 10* tested the lunar module, the spacecraft that would land on the Moon, but did not make an actual landing. After three successful manned test flights, the program was ready to try for a landing with *Apollo 11*.

The first landing on the Moon would indeed be a

The command module, shown here in Moon orbit, was first tested by Apollo 8 astronauts. This module carried three astronauts into orbit, but did not land on its surface.

great adventure. The effort to put astronauts on the Moon began in 1961, when President John F. Kennedy challenged the United States space program to land an astronaut on the Moon before the end of the 1960s. The United States and the Soviet Union had a tense relationship during that time. Both nations' space programs were trying to get their astronauts to the Moon first. The first nation that put its astronauts on the Moon would enhance its political status in the world and prove its technical superiority.

But there were also many scientific reasons for sending astronauts to the Moon. By allowing astronauts to bring back Moon rocks for scientists to study, the lunar missions could help answer questions about where the Moon came from and how it was formed.

Apollo 11 made its historic landing on the Moon on

July 20, 1969. The astronauts returned to Earth with forty-eight pounds of the important lunar rock samples scientists had been waiting for. The astronauts also placed experimental equipment on the Moon. They included a seismometer to measure "moonquakes," and a special mirror device that reflected laser beams from Earth to measure the exact distance to the Moon.

Five more Moon-landing missions followed *Apollo 11*. *Apollo 15* marked the first use of the Lunar Roving Vehicle. It allowed astronauts to travel further across the

After the first successful orbit of the Moon, Apollo 8's *command module splashed down into the Pacific Ocean.*

A footprint from an Apollo 11 *astronaut marks man's first visit to the Moon.*

surface from their Lunar Module lander. In all, the six Apollo missions brought back 842 pounds of lunar rocks. Scientists began studying the rocks immediately, looking for answers about the Moon's origin.

Prior to the Apollo missions, scientists believed there were three possible explanations for the Moon's origin. Some believed the Moon and Earth had formed at the same time from the same gas and dust present in the early solar system. Others believed that during Earth's early molten phase the planet's spin had been great enough to throw a large chunk of material out into space to form the Moon. The third idea was that the Moon had formed somewhere else in the solar system and was later captured when it wandered too close to Earth's gravity. Moon rock samples brought back by the Apollo astronauts would help tell scientists which one of these ideas might be right.[2]

The Lunar Rocks

Scientists studying the lunar rocks discovered many similarities between them and the rock found in Earth's mantle. The similarities made scientists think Earth and the Moon were formed in the same part of the early solar system. But the differences in the rock challenged their earlier thoughts about the Moon's formation.

The astronauts of Apollo 11 examine the Moon rocks they collected during their mission. After studying the rocks, scientists discovered that there were many similarities between the Moon rocks and the rock in Earth's mantle.

These differences are very significant. The Moon rocks showed fewer elements that melt at low temperatures and far greater amounts of other elements that remain solid at higher temperatures. This evidence suggested that a very hot, violent event had occurred in the Moon's history, resulting in the Moon's forming in a way very different from the way Earth was formed.[3]

Such evidence began to unravel earlier theories. If the Moon and Earth had formed at the same time and place, their rocks should be more similar. They would also be similar if the Moon had once been part of Earth. But if the Moon had been formed in another part of the early solar system (where it was either much colder or much hotter), the rock samples should be more different.

The Moon's Origin

The Apollo Moon rock samples forced scientists to consider a new theory of the Moon's origin. The current theory proposes that an object the size of Mars (approximately 4,000 miles wide) struck Earth about 4.6 billion years ago. The impact vaporized nearly all of the impact-object's mantle and part of Earth's mantle. The exposed metal core of the impact-object was then absorbed through Earth's upper mantle to become an added part of Earth's core.

The giant impact blasted great amounts of both Earth's and the impact-object's mantles into space. The heat of the blast had vaporized water and some other

Apollo expeditions to the Moon helped scientists consider new theories about how the Moon was formed.

elements. Only the materials that remain solid at higher temperatures retained their structure through the heat of the blast to be thrown out into orbit around Earth. Scientists believe the material collapsed into a disk around Earth shortly after the impact. It clumped into the object that became our Moon within just a few years.[4]

The giant-impact explanation has not been proven. Scientists do not know for sure how or where the Moon was formed. This latest theory simply offers the best explanation so far for what we currently know about the Moon's properties.

Clementine and Lunar Prospector

The *Clementine* spacecraft made a more detailed survey of the lunar surface in 1994. *Clementine* was the first spacecraft to visit the Moon since the last Soviet Luna probe in the mid-1970s.

Our knowledge of the Moon continued to expand with the help of NASA's *Lunar Prospector*. Launched to the Moon in 1998, *Lunar Prospector* took measurements of the Moon's gravitational and magnetic fields, and searched for traces of certain gases, minerals, and deposits of water ice.

"The Moon is close to home," said *Lunar Prospector* scientist Rick Elphic, "but it's still a foreign land, an alien province." Elphic was one of the scientists searching for answers that might reveal a better picture of the Moon's mysterious history. "It seems so simple," he said, "yet *Lunar Prospector* has shown that its history is remarkably complex."[5]

Using an instrument called a magnetometer, *Lunar Prospector* took magnetic readings that showed the Moon's metal core made up 4 percent or less of the Moon's total mass. Earth's metal core makes up nearly one-third of its mass. This evidence of a much smaller metal core within the Moon fit well with the large-impact theory of the Moon's origin.

"We have known for a long time that the Moon is depleted in metals," said *Lunar Prospector* scientist Lon L. Hood. "But the new measurements tell us more accurately how depleted it is. It is extremely depleted."[6]

Earth and other bodies in the solar system took form when smaller objects clumped together over millions of years to form larger ones. As the clumping caused the young Earth's size to increase, its interior became heated. Heavier metals, such as iron, melted and sank to the center, forming a large metal core.

Lunar Prospector's measurements of only a tiny core within the Moon are an "indicator that the Moon had a unique origin," according to Hood. A past event such as the giant impact described by scientists may have caused the Moon to form with such a small core.[7]

Another instrument called a neutron spectrometer aboard *Lunar Prospector* discovered what appeared to be water ice at the Moon's north and south poles. Each time the spacecraft orbited over the polar regions, the instrument detected large deposits of hydrogen, which is a major component of water. Scientists believe that the water ice exists within constantly shadowed areas at the poles. Some steep crater walls at the Moon's poles form shadows that have kept parts of the lunar surface completely hidden from sunlight for billions of years. According to scientists, the suspected ice in these shadows collected there after the impacts of comets on the Moon. The theory states that billions of years of micrometeorite impacts have mixed the ice into the regolith dust. With no sunlight reaching these shadowed areas, the ice was never melted or evaporated by the Sun.[8]

The suspected ice deposits in these shadows are huge. Up to 75 billion gallons of water may be frozen in the top few inches of lunar dust in these craters. But the existence of the water ice has not yet been proven.

When *Lunar Prospector* had completed its mission, it was commanded to crash into one of these craters. Scientists hoped that the heat created by the crash would melt part of the ice and produce a cloud of water vapor. Then they could observe the cloud by telescopes from Earth, confirming the existence of water ice at the Moon's poles. Unfortunately, no cloud of vapor was detected. This could mean that there is no ice at the poles, that the ice was too deep to be disturbed by the crash, or that the spacecraft missed the targeted area. No one knows for certain.

Scientists are still very interested to learn if there is water ice in these areas because the presence of water ice on the Moon could prove very useful. Quantities of such water will be important to any future human outposts or bases on the Moon.[9]

Nearly thirty years have passed since the last human walked on the lunar surface. NASA is making plans to return there in the near future. Equipment is being designed and missions are being planned that will return humans to the Moon sometime in the first or second decade of the twenty-first century. Maybe you will be one of the lucky astronauts who will go on one of those missions. Until then, you can use your imagination to go to the Moon.

5

Observing the Moon, from Near and Far

Walking on the Moon is an interesting and enjoyable experience. Ask any astronaut who has been there.

"You just stand out there and say, 'I don't believe what I'm looking at!'" said Eugene Cernan of *Apollo 17*.[1]

Apollo 11's Edwin Aldrin described his first view of the Moon's landscape as "magnificent desolation."[2]

The lifeless, desolate quality of the lunar surface was not all that challenged the astronauts' senses. The incredibly black sky above the Moon made their surroundings seem truly alien.

"Most people can't comprehend a black sky except at night," said *Apollo 15*'s David Scott. Astronauts on the Moon, he explained, see a black sky in the daytime. "When the surface of the Moon is illuminated, and it's bright, there are shadows, and contrasts . . . And above that it is a black sky—that is a whole new thing for the mind to handle."[3]

Their bodies had to handle the new experience of the Moon's gravity. The Moon has only one-sixth the gravity of Earth. The average astronaut, dressed in his complete Moonwalking spacesuit, weighed 360 pounds

Astronaut Eugene Cernan cruised around the Moon's surface in the Lunar Roving Vehicle.

(164 kilograms) on Earth. On the Moon, he weighed only 60 pounds (27 kilograms).

If you, a young person, went to the Moon, you might weigh 250 pounds (114 kilograms) in your spacesuit. But you would weigh only 42 pounds (20 kilograms) on the Moon. It might take time to find your balance in this lighter gravity, but once you did, you would be bouncing along the surface with ease. Most astronauts found it easier to do a sort of hopping motion to get from place to place. The regular style of walking was too awkward in the bulky spacesuits and lighter gravity. When the astronauts wanted to cross some open territory, they hopped.

The next thing you would notice is that the day goes on and on. The Sun would not appear to rise and set every 24 hours as it does on Earth. Because the Moon rotates on its axis only once every 27 1/2 Earth days, a "day" on the Moon would last almost two weeks. The night would last just as long.

During this very long night, you would experience the beauty of seeing Earth become gradually illuminated by the Sun. As the Moon continued around Earth in its orbit, more and more of the Earth would become lit by the Sun, until it was a blue-and-white globe in the darkness of space.

For now, you can instead look up at the Moon and its phases in the more familiar skies of Earth. But the Moon's phases are not the only interaction between sunlight and the Moon you can observe. Sometimes the Moon causes a spectacular event called an eclipse.

A solar eclipse occurs when the Moon passes directly between the Sun and Earth. As the Moon blocks the Sun's light, it casts a shadow across a small area of Earth about 100 miles (260 kilometers) wide. Only the people in this small area will see the total eclipse. Those outside the small area will see the Sun's light only partially blocked by the Moon.

Although the time of total eclipse usually lasts only a few minutes, it is a spectacular few minutes. During that time, the Moon appears as a black disc, surrounded by a blazing ring of sunlight called the corona. People witnessing the eclipse feel the air temperature around them drop rapidly. A dull, eerie kind

Astronaut Alan Bean spends some time in his spacesuit while practicing in a lunar surface training machine. The machine imitates the one-sixth gravity conditions on the Moon.

of light invades the area. It is an odd twilight, like neither dawn nor dusk. Birds and other animals go strangely quiet, confused by what seems the early coming of nightfall. This brief blockage of the Sun's light indeed creates a spectacle of nature unlike any other.

A solar eclipse occurs somewhere on Earth once every year or so. Some people travel around the world to the site of an eclipse in order to experience this breathtaking event.[4]

Another kind of eclipse is a lunar eclipse. This occurs when the Moon reaches a position in its orbit that places Earth directly between the Sun and the Moon. In this alignment, Earth blocks the light from the Sun and casts its shadow across the face of the Moon. Over a period of hours, the Moon grows slowly darker as Earth's shadow falls across the lunar surface. The shadow upon the Moon may appear various shades of red or orange. The color results from the Sun's light being bent as it passes through Earth's atmosphere. The color of light that falls on the Moon then appears red or orange, similar to the way the Sun's light appears on Earth during sunrise or sunset.[5]

The reason that eclipses do not happen more often is that the Moon orbits Earth at a slight angle. Although the Moon crosses between the Sun and Earth twelve times each year (in some years, thirteen), most often it passes either slightly above or slightly below the Sun.

Only when the Moon and Earth move into positions of exact alignment with the Sun does an eclipse occur.

Observing the Moon from night to night as it progresses through its phases is an enjoyable activity. During the time between the Moon's First Quarter and Full Moon phases, see how early in the evening you can spot the Moon. You may be able to spot it in the sky hours before sunset. At Full Moon, the Moon rises from the eastern horizon at the same time that the Sun is setting in the west. This makes sense, since the Moon can appear full only when it reaches a position in space on the opposite side of Earth from the Sun.

A lunar eclipse occurs when Earth casts a shadow on the Moon. This lunar eclipse was photographed from Florida on January 20, 2000.

After the Full Moon phase of the Moon's cycle, the Moon rises above the eastern horizon later and later after sunset. To see the Moon during this part of its cycle, you have to stay up later each night. When the sky is very clear, this phase of the Moon is often visible in the western sky throughout the morning hours of daylight.[6]

Because it is so near, the Moon is one of the most interesting objects in the sky to observe. Some of the largest craters on the Moon can be seen with the naked eye. Use a telescope or a pair of binoculars to observe much more in amazing detail. Although you can look at the Moon with a pair of binoculars or telescope, **never look directly at the Sun**. It can cause permanent eye damage.

The best time to observe the Moon is when part of it is in shadow. The line separating the dark from the lighted side of the Moon at any time is called the terminator. Shadows along the terminator create interesting contrasts that allow you to see more detail in the cratered lunar surface. You can then look at a map or atlas of the Moon to see the names of some of the craters you are observing. Most are named after famous astronomers and scientists.[7]

Its bright light and changing phases make the Moon hard to ignore in our night skies. In the past forty years, we have learned much about it, and have even traveled there. But all our recent knowledge and thousands of years of wondering have not dimmed our fascination with the Moon.

CHAPTER NOTES

Chapter 1. One Small Step
1. Apollo 11, *Technical Air-to-Ground Voice Transcription*, Manned Spacecraft Center, Houston, Texas, July 1969.

Chapter 2. Earth's Companion
1. Patrick Moore, *The Moon* (New York: Rand McNally and Company, 1981), p. 5.
2. Ibid.
3. J. Kelly Beatty, Carolyn Petersen, and Andrew Chaikin. *The New Solar System* (Cambridge, Mass.: Sky Publishing Corporation, 1999), pp. 134–136.
4. Beatty, Petersen, and Chaikin, pp. 126–128.
5. Jean Audouze and Guy Israel, eds., *The Cambridge Atlas of Astronomy* (Cambridge, Eng.: Cambridge University Press, 1996), pp. 106–113.
6. Beatty, Petersen, and Chaikin, p. 71.
7. Audouze and Israel, pp. 106–109.
8. Michael Light, *Full Moon* (New York: Alfred A. Knopf, Inc., 1999), p. 172.

Moon Chart
Antonin Rukl, *Atlas of the Moon* (Waukesha, Wis.: Kalmbach Publishing Company, 1996), pp. 7–19.

Chapter 3. Tides, Orbit, and Phases of the Moon
1. Antonin Rukl, *Atlas of the Moon* (Waukesha, Wis.: Kalmback Publishing Company, 1996), p. 7.
2. Bob Berman, *Secrets of the Night Sky* (New York: William Morrow and Company, Inc., 1995), pp. 143, 270.
3. Patrick Moore, *The Moon* (New York: Rand McNally and Company, 1981), pp. 8–9.

Chapter 4. Journeys to the Moon

1. Patrick Moore, *The Moon* (New York: Rand McNally and Company, 1981), p. 14.

2. Jean Audouze and Guy Israel, eds., *The Cambridge Atlas of Astronomy* (Cambridge, Eng.: Cambridge University Press, 1996), p. 105.

3. J. Kelly Beatty, Carolyn Petersen, and Andrew Chaikin, *The New Solar System* (Cambridge, Mass.: Sky Publishing Corporation, 1999), p. 137.

4. Ibid., pp. 137–138.

5. Robert Irion, "Raising Lunar Prospects," *Astronomy*, February 2000, p. 51.

6. Kenneth Silber, "Magnetic Data Hint at Moon's Unique Origin," *Science: Solar System—The Moon*, August 10, 1999, <http://www.space.com/science/solarsystem/moon_core.html> (January 6, 2000).

7. Ibid.

8. Irion, p. 46.

9. Ibid.

Chapter 5. Observing the Moon, from Near and Far

1. Michael Light, *Full Moon* (New York: Alfred A. Knopf, Inc., 1999), p. 171.

2. Apollo 11, *Technical Air-to-Ground Voice Transcription*, Manned Spacecraft Center, Houston, Texas, July 1969.

3. Light, p. 171.

4. Terence Dickinson, *Nightwatch: A Practical Guide to Viewing the Universe*, 3rd ed. (New York: Firefly Books, Inc., 1998), pp. 146–150.

5. Antonin Rukl, *Atlas of the Moon* (Waukesha, Wis.: Kalmbach Publishing Company, 1996), pp. 213–214.

6. Ibid., p. 11.

7. Ibid., pp. 208–210.

GLOSSARY

basalt—Rock formed by volcanic activity.

core—The center of the Moon, which lies beneath the crust and mantle layers. Scientists believe the Moon's core makes up less than 3 percent of its mass and is made of iron.

crust—The Moon's rocky outer layer. It covers the mantle, and is twenty to sixty miles thick.

First Quarter Moon—The Moon phase about seven days after New Moon, when the right half of the Moon appears illuminated.

Full Moon—The Moon phase about fifteen days after New Moon, when the entire face of the Moon appears illuminated. The Full Moon rises in the east as the Sun is setting in the west.

lunar eclipse—An event that occurs when the Moon orbits to a position that places Earth directly between the Sun and the Moon. In this alignment, Earth blocks the Sun's light and casts a shadow across the Moon.

mantle—The deep, inner layer of the Moon that lies below the crust. The mantle layer probably makes up 90 percent of the Moon's mass.

maria—The darker, smoother areas of the Moon's surface that have fewer craters. *Mare* is the singular.

micrometeorites—The tiny bits of dust and debris that are constantly impacting the surface of the Moon from space. These tiny meteorites are the kind that appear as "shooting stars" when they burn up because of friction with Earth's atmosphere. The Moon has no atmosphere to burn them up.

New Moon—The Moon phase when the side of the Moon facing Earth is completely unlit by the Sun, and cannot be seen from Earth.

orbit—The path that a body in space takes around another body in space as a result of gravitational forces.

regolith—The fine, gray dust completely covering the Moon's surface. It was created by billions of years of micrometeorite impacts pounding the lunar rocks into dust.

sidereal month—The 27-day-and-8-hour period that it takes for the Moon to complete one orbit of Earth.

solar eclipse—The event that occurs when the Moon's orbit carries it to a position directly between the Sun and Earth. This alignment causes the Moon to block the Sun's light and cast a shadow across a small area of Earth.

synodic month—The 29-and-a-half-day period required for the Moon to complete its cycle of phases, from New Moon to the next New Moon.

terminator—The boundary between light and shadow that separates day and night on the Moon at any given time. The contrast of light and shadow in the terminator area makes it one of the most interesting areas to observe through a telescope.

terrae—The mountainous highland areas of the Moon's surface. The terrae are rougher than the maria, and have many more craters.

Third Quarter Moon—The Moon phase about 22 days after New Moon, in which the entire eastern, or left, half of the Moon appears illuminated.

FURTHER READING

Books

Cole, Michael. *Moon Base: First Colony in Space*. Springfield, N.J.: Enslow Publishers, Inc., 1999.

Estalella, Robert. *Our Satellite: The Moon*. New York: Barron's Educational Series, Inc., 1994.

Gardner, Robert. *Science Project Ideas About the Moon*. Springfield, N.J.: Enslow Publishers, Inc., 1997.

Kustenmacher, Werner. *Frommer's The Moon: A Guide for First Time Visitors*. Indianapolis: Macmillan General Reference, 1999.

Rukl, Antonin. *Atlas of the Moon*. Waukesha, Wis.: Kalmbach Publishing Company, 1996.

Vogt, Gregory L. *Apollo Moonwalks: The Amazing Lunar Missions*. Springfield, N.J.: Enslow Publishers, Inc., 2000.

Internet Addresses

Arnett, Bill. *The Nine Planets Tour—The Moon*. September 15, 2000. <http://www.seds.org/nineplanets/nineplanets/luna.html> (October 6, 2000).

Invitation to the Moon. January 16, 2000 <http://www.sutv.zaq.ne.jp/ckabp800/moon/> (October 6, 2000).

Lunar and Planetary Institute. Exploring the Moon. © 2000. <http://cass.jsc.nasa.gov/moon.html> (October 6, 2000).

INDEX